"I'm selfish, impatient and a little insecure. I make mistakes, I am out of control and at times hard to handle. But if you can't handle me at my worst, then you sure as hell don't deserve me at my best."
— Marilyn Monroe

"You've gotta dance
like there's nobody watching,
Love like you'll never be hurt,
Sing like there's nobody listening,
And live like it's heaven on earth."
— William W. Purkey

"You know you're in love when you can't fall asleep because reality is finally better than your dreams."
— Dr. Seuss

"A friend is someone who knows all about you
and still loves you."
— Elbert Hubbard

"Darkness cannot drive out darkness: only light can
do that. Hate cannot drive out hate:
only love can do that."
— Martin Luther King Jr.

"We accept the love we think we deserve."
— Stephen Chbosky,

"It is better to be hated for what you are than to be
loved for what you are not."
— André Gide

"As he read, I fell in love the way you fall asleep: slowly, and then all at once."
— *John Green*

"The opposite of love is not hate, it's indifference. The opposite of art is not ugliness, it's indifference. The opposite of faith is not heresy, it's indifference. And the opposite of life is not death, it's indifference."
— *Elie Wiesel*

"It is not a lack of love, but a lack of friendship that makes unhappy marriages."
— *Friedrich Nietzsche*

---

"I love you without knowing how, or when, or from where. I love you simply, without problems or pride: I love you in this way because I do not know any other way of loving but this, in which there is no I or you, so intimate that your hand upon my chest is my hand, so intimate that when
I fall asleep your eyes close."
— *Pablo Neruda*

"Have you ever been in love? Horrible isn't it? It makes you so vulnerable. It opens your chest and it opens up your heart and it means that someone can get inside you and mess you up."
— *Neil Gaiman*

"Love all, trust a few, do wrong to none."
—William Shakespeare

---

"Being deeply loved by someone gives you strength, while loving someone deeply gives you courage."
— Lao Tzu

"There is never a time or place for true love. It happens accidentally, in a heartbeat, in a single flashing, throbbing moment."
— Sarah Dessen

"Love is that condition in which the happiness of another person is essential to your own."
— Robert A. Heinlein

"You love me. Real or not real?"
I tell him, "Real."
— Suzanne Collins

---

I am nothing special, of this I am sure. I am a common man with common thoughts and I've led a common life. There are no monuments dedicated to me and my name will soon be forgotten, but I've loved another with all my heart and soul, and to me, this has always been enough.."
— Nicholas Sparks

"Love looks not with the eyes, but with the mind,
And therefore is winged Cupid painted blind."
— William Shakespeare

"Love is like the wind, you can't see it but you can feel it."
— Nicholas Sparks

"If you can make a woman laugh, you can make her do anything."
— Marilyn Monroe

"You don't love someone because they're perfect, you love them in spite of the fact that they're not."
— Jodi Picoult

"We're all a little weird. And life is a little weird. And when we find someone whose weirdness is compatible with ours, we join up with them and fall into mutually satisfying weirdness — and call it love — true love."
— Robert Fulghum

"Love never dies a natural death. It dies because we don't know how to replenish its source. It dies of blindness and errors and betrayals. It dies of illness and wounds; it dies of weariness, of witherings, of tarnishings."
— Anaïs Nin

---

"There is nothing I would not do for those who are really my friends. I have no notion of loving people by halves, it is not my nature."
— Jane Austen

"The real lover is the man who can thrill you by kissing your forehead or smiling into your eyes or just staring into space."
— Marilyn Monroe

"If I had a flower for every time I thought of you...I could walk through my garden forever."
— Alfred Tennyson

"When someone loves you, the way they talk about you is different. You feel safe and comfortable."
— Jess C. Scott

"To love at all is to be vulnerable. Love anything and your heart will be wrung and possibly broken. If you want to make sure of keeping it intact you must give it to no one, not even an animal. Wrap it carefully round with hobbies and little luxuries; avoid all entanglements. Lock it up safe in the casket or coffin of your selfishness. But in that casket, safe, dark, motionless, airless, it will change. It will not be broken; it will become unbreakable, impenetrable, irredeemable. To love is to be vulnerable."
— C.S. Lewis

"Dumbledore watched her fly away, and as her silvery glow faded he turned back to Snape, and his eyes were full of tears.
"After all this time?"
"Always," said Snape."
— J.K. Rowling

"I've been making a list of the things they don't teach you at school. They don't teach you how to love somebody. They don't teach you how to be famous. They don't teach you how to be rich or how to be poor. They don't teach you how to walk away from someone you don't love any longer. They don't teach you how to know what's going on in someone else's mind. They don't teach you what to say to someone who's dying.
They don't teach you anything worth knowing."
— Neil Gaiman

"To die will be an awfully big adventure."
— J.M. Barrie

"A lady's imagination is very rapid; it jumps from admiration to love, from love to matrimony in a moment."
—Jane Austen

---

"So it's not gonna be easy. It's going to be really hard;
we're gonna have to work at this everyday, but I
want to do that because I want you. I want all of you,
forever, everyday. You and me... everyday."
— Nicholas Sparks

"Just when you think it can't get any worse, it can.
And just when you think it can't get any better, it
can."
— Nicholas Sparks

"Tis better to have loved and lost
Than never to have loved at all."
— Alfred Tennyson

"I love you as certain dark things are to be loved,
in secret, between the shadow and the soul."
— Pablo Neruda

"He's not perfect. You aren't either, and the two of you will never be perfect. But if he can make you laugh at least once, causes you to think twice, and if he admits to being human and making mistakes, hold onto him and give him the most you can. He isn't going to quote poetry, he's not thinking about you every moment, but he will give you a part of him that he knows you could break. Don't hurt him, don't change him, and don't expect for more than he can give. Don't analyze. Smile when he makes you happy, yell when he makes you mad, and miss him when he's not there. Love hard when there is love to be had. Because perfect guys don't exist, but there's always one guy that is perfect for you."
— Bob Marley

"The one you love and the one who loves you are never, ever the same person."
— Chuck Palahniuk

"Some people don't understand the promises they're making when they make them," I said.
"Right, of course. But you keep the promise anyway. That's what love is. Love is keeping the promise anyway."
— John Green

"Love is needing someone. Love is putting up with someone's bad qualities because they somehow complete you."
— Sarah Dessen

*"So, I love you because the entire universe conspired to help me find you."*
— Paulo Coelho

"I no longer believed in the idea of soul mates, or love at first sight. But I was beginning to believe that a very few times in your life, if you were lucky, you might meet someone who was exactly right for you. Not because he was perfect, or because you were, but because your combined flaws were arranged in a way that allowed two separate beings to hinge together."
— Lisa Kleypas

"When I despair, I remember that all through history the way of truth and love have always won. There have been tyrants and murderers, and for a time, they can seem invincible, but in the end, they always fall. Think of it--always."
— Mahatma Gandhi

"One is loved because one is loved. No reason is needed for loving."
—*Paulo Coelho*

"When we love, we always strive to become better than we are. When we strive to become better than we are, everything around us becomes better too."
— Paulo Coelho

"Love is patient, love is kind. It does not envy, it does not boast, it is not proud. It is not rude, it is not self-seeking, it is not easily angered, it keeps no record of wrongs. Love does not delight in evil but rejoices with the truth. It always protects, always trusts, always hopes, always perseveres."
— Anonymous

"We love the things we love for what they are."
— Robert Frost

"I would die for you. But I won't live for you."
— Stephen Chbosky

---

"In vain have I struggled. It will not do. My feelings will not be repressed. You must allow me to tell you how ardently I admire and love you."
— Jane Austen

"Perhaps all the dragons in our lives are princesses who are only waiting to see us act, just once, with beauty and courage. Perhaps everything that frightens us is, in its deepest essence, something helpless that wants our love."
— Rainer Maria Rilke

"You are, and always have been, my dream."
— Nicholas Sparks

"You are my best friend as well as my lover, and I do not know which side of you I enjoy the most. I treasure each side, just as I have treasured our life together."
— Nicholas Sparks

"I carry your heart with me (I carry it in my heart)I
am never without it (anywhere
I go you go,my dear; and whatever is done by only
me is your doing,my darling)
I fear no fate (for you are my fate,my sweet)I want no
world (for beautiful you are my world,my true)
and it's you are whatever a moon has always meant
and whatever a sun will always sing is you

here is the deepest secret nobody knows
(here is the root of the root and the bud of the bud
and the sky of the sky of a tree called life; which
grows
higher than the soul can hope or mind can hide)
and this is the wonder that's keeping the stars apart

I carry your heart (I carry it in my heart)"
— E.E. Cummings

"The only thing worse than a boy who hates you: a
boy that loves you."
— Markus Zusak

---

"And now I'm looking at you," he said, "and you're asking me if I still want you, as if I could stop loving you. As if I would want to give up the thing that makes me stronger than anything else ever has. I never dared give much of myself to anyone before – bits of myself to the Lightwoods, to Isabelle and Alec, but it took years to do it – but, Clary, since the first time I saw you, I have belonged to you completely. I still do. If you want me."
— Cassandra Clare


"Where there is love there is life."
—Mahatma Gandhi


"Never love anyone who treats you like you're ordinary."
— Oscar Wilde


"I would always rather be happy than dignified."
—*Charlotte Brontë*

---

"Promise Yourself
To be so strong that nothing
can disturb your peace of mind.
To talk health, happiness, and prosperity
to every person you meet.
To make all your friends feel
that there is something in them
To look at the sunny side of everything
and make your optimism come true.
To think only the best, to work only for the best,
and to expect only the best.
To be just as enthusiastic about the success of others
as you are about your own.
To forget the mistakes of the past
and press on to the greater achievements of the
future.
To wear a cheerful countenance at all times
and give every living creature you meet a smile.
To give so much time to the improvement of yourself
that you have no time to criticize others.
To be too large for worry, too noble for anger, too
strong for fear,
and too happy to permit the presence of trouble.
To think well of yourself and to proclaim this fact to
the world,
not in loud words but great deeds.
To live in faith that the whole world is on your side
so long as you are true to the best that is in you."

— Christian D. Larson

---

"Life will break you. Nobody can protect you from that, and living alone won't either, for solitude will also break you with its yearning. You have to love. You have to feel. It is the reason you are here on earth. You are here to risk your heart. You are here to be swallowed up. And when it happens that you are broken, or betrayed, or left, or hurt, or death brushes near, let yourself sit by an apple tree and listen to the apples falling all around you in heaps, wasting their sweetness. Tell yourself you tasted as many as you could."
— Louise Erdrich


"Once upon a time there was a boy who loved a girl, and her laughter was a question he wanted to spend his whole life answering."
— Nicole Krauss


"Nobody has ever measured, not even poets, how much the heart can hold."
— Zelda Fitzgerald

---

"The best love is the kind that awakens the soul and makes us reach for more, that plants a fire in our hearts and brings peace to our minds. And that's what you've given me. That's what I'd hoped to give you forever"
— Nicholas Sparks

"There are two basic motivating forces: fear and love. When we are afraid, we pull back from life. When we are in love, we open to all that life has to offer with passion, excitement, and acceptance. We need to learn to love ourselves first, in all our glory and our imperfections. If we cannot love ourselves, we cannot fully open to our ability to love others or our potential to create. Evolution and all hopes for a better world rest in the fearlessness and open-hearted vision of people who embrace life."
—John Lennon

"We loved with a love that was more than love."
— Edgar Allan Poe

"We fell in love, despite our differences, and once we did, something rare and beautiful was created. For me, love like that has only happened once, and that's why every minute we spent together has been seared in my memory. I'll never forget a single moment of it."
— Nicholas Sparks

"Some women choose to follow men, and some women choose to follow their dreams. If you're wondering which way to go, remember that your career will never wake up and tell you that it doesn't love you anymore."
— Lady Gaga

"I think you still love me, but we can't escape the fact that I'm not enough for you. I knew this was going to happen. So I'm not blaming you for falling in love with another woman. I'm not angry, either. I should be, but I'm not. I just feel pain. A lot of pain. I thought I could imagine how much this would hurt, but I was wrong."
— Haruki Murakami

---

"And so the lion fell in love with the lamb…" he
murmured. I looked away, hiding my eyes as I
thrilled to the word.
"What a stupid lamb," I sighed.
"What a sick, masochistic lion."
— Stephenie Meyer

"This is a good sign, having a broken heart. It means
we have tried for something."
— Elizabeth Gilbert

"Every heart sings a song, incomplete, until another
heart whispers back. Those who wish to sing always
find a song. At the touch of a lover, everyone
becomes a poet."
— Plato

---

"Doubt thou the stars are fire;
Doubt that the sun doth move;
Doubt truth to be a liar;
But never doubt I love."
— William Shakespeare

"I heard what you said. I'm not the silly romantic
you think. I don't want the heavens or the shooting
stars. I don't want gemstones or gold. I have those
things already. I want…a steady hand. A kind soul. I
want to fall asleep, and wake, knowing my heart is
safe. I want to love, and be loved."
— Shana Abe

"A guy and a girl can be just friends, but at one point
or another, they will fall for each other...Maybe
temporarily, maybe at the wrong time, maybe too
late, or maybe forever"
— Dave Matthews Band

"The more I know of the world, the more I am convinced that I shall never see a man whom I can really love. I require so much!"
— Jane Austen

"Eleanor was right. She never looked nice. She looked like art, and art wasn't supposed to look nice; it was supposed to make you feel something."
— Rainbow Rowell

"He's more myself than I am. Whatever our souls are made of, his and mine are the same."
— Emily Brontë

"What's meant to be will always find a way"
— Trisha Yearwood

---

"I have decided to stick to love...Hate is too great a
burden to bear."
— Martin Luther King Jr.

"Above all, don't lie to yourself. The man who lies to
himself and listens to his own lie comes to a point
that he cannot distinguish the truth within him, or
around him, and so loses all respect for himself and
for others. And having no respect he ceases to love."
— Fyodor Dostoyevsky

"Out beyond ideas of wrongdoing
and rightdoing there is a field.
I'll meet you there.
When the soul lies down in that grass
the world is too full to talk about."
— Jalaluddin Rumi

"Everyone, at some point in their lives, wakes up in the middle of the night with the feeling that they are all alone in the world, and that nobody loves them now and that nobody will ever love them, and that they will never have a decent night's sleep again and will spend their lives wandering blearily around a loveless landscape, hoping desperately that their circumstances will improve, but suspecting, in their heart of hearts, that they will remain unloved forever. The best thing to do in these circumstances is to wake somebody else up,
so that they can feel this way, too."
— Lemony Snicket

"They say a person needs just three things to be truly happy in this world: someone to love, something to do, and something to hope for."
— Tom Bodett

"Two people in love, alone, isolated from the world, that's beautiful."
— Milan Kundera

"No relationship is perfect, ever. There are always some ways you have to bend, to compromise, to give something up in order to gain something greater...The love we have for each other is bigger than these small differences. And that's the key. It's like a big pie chart, and the love in a relationship has to be the biggest piece. Love can make up for a lot."
— Sarah Dessen

"The heart was made to be broken."
— Oscar Wilde

"Love is always patient and kind. It is never jealous. Love is never boastful or conceited. It is never rude or selfish. It does not take offense and is not resentful. Love takes no pleasure in other people's sins, but delights in the truth. It is always ready to excuse, to trust, to hope, and to endure whatever comes."
— Anonymous

---

"We live and breathe words. .... It was books that made me feel that perhaps I was not completely alone. They could be honest with me, and I with them. Reading your words, what you wrote, how you were lonely sometimes and afraid, but always brave; the way you saw the world, its colors and textures and sounds, I felt--I felt the way you thought, hoped, felt, dreamt. I felt I was dreaming and thinking and feeling *with* you. I dreamed what you dreamed, wanted what you wanted--and then I realized that truly I just wanted you."
— Cassandra Clare

"This above all: to thine own self be true,
And it must follow, as the night the day,
Thou canst not then be false to any man."
— William Shakespeare

"I have a history of making decisions very quickly about men. I have always fallen in love fast and without measuring risks. I have a tendency not only to see the best in everyone, but to assume that everyone is emotionally capable of reaching his highest potential. I have fallen in love more times than I care to count with the highest potential of a man, rather than with the man himself, and I have hung on to the relationship for a long time (sometimes far too long) waiting for the man to ascend to his own greatness. Many times in romance I have been a victim of my own optimism."
— Elizabeth Gilbert

"For the two of us, home isn't a place. It is a person. And we are finally home."
— Stephanie Perkins

"Love is so short, forgetting is so long."
— Pablo Neruda

"You could have had anything else in the world, and you asked for me."
She smiled up at him. Filthy as he was, covered in blood and dirt, he was the most beautiful thing she'd ever seen.
"But I don't want anything else in the world."
— Cassandra Clare

"They didn't agree on much. In fact, they didn't agree on anything. They fought all the time and challenged each other ever day. But despite their differences, they had one important thing in common. They were crazy about each other."
— Nicholas Sparks

"Have you ever been in love? Horrible isn't it? It makes you so vulnerable. It opens your chest and it opens up your heart and it means that someone can get inside you and mess you up. You build up all these defenses, you build up a whole suit of armor, so that nothing can hurt you, then one stupid person, no different from any other stupid person, wanders into your stupid life...You give them a piece of you. They didn't ask for it. They did something dumb one day, like kiss you or smile at you, and then your life isn't your own anymore. Love takes hostages. It gets inside you. It eats you out and leaves you crying in the darkness, so simple a phrase like 'maybe we should be just friends' turns into a glass splinter working its way into your heart. It hurts. Not just in the imagination. Not just in the mind. It's a soul-hurt, a real gets-inside-you-and-rips-you-apart pain. I hate love."
— Neil Gaiman

"I think if I've learned anything about friendship, it's to hang in, stay connected, fight for them, and let them fight for you. Don't walk away, don't be distracted, don't be too busy or tired, don't take them for granted. Friends are part of the glue that holds life and faith together. Powerful stuff."
— Jon Katz

"To douchebags!" he said, gesturing to Brad. "And to girls that break your heart," he bowed his head to me. His eyes lost focus. " And to the absolute fucking horror of losing your best friend because you were stupid enough to fall in love with her."
— Jamie McGuire

"The world is indeed full of peril, and in it there are many dark places; but still there is much that is fair, and though in all lands love is now mingled with grief, it grows perhaps the greater."
— J.R.R. Tolkien

"The very essence of romance is uncertainty."
— Oscar Wilde

"What I want is to be needed. What I need is to be indispensable to somebody. Who I need is somebody that will eat up all my free time, my ego, my attention. Somebody addicted to me. A mutual addiction."
— Chuck Palahniuk

"There is always some madness in love. But there is also always some reason in madness."
— Friedrich Nietzsche

"If all else perished, and he remained, I should still continue to be; and if all else remained, and he were annihilated, the universe would turn to a mighty stranger."
— Emily Brontë

---

"My daddy said, that the first time you fall in love, it changes you forever and no matter how hard you try, that feeling just never goes away."
— Nicholas Sparks

"Man may have discovered fire, but women discovered how to play with it."
— Candace Bushnell

"And, in the end
The love you take
is equal to the love you make."
— Paul McCartney

"What I need is the dandelion in the spring.The bright yellow that means rebirth instead of destruction. The promise that life can go on, no matter how bad our losses.
That it can be good again."
— Suzanne Collins

---

"It hurts to let go. Sometimes it seems the harder you try to hold on to something or someone the more it wants to get away. You feel like some kind of criminal for having felt, for having wanted. For having wanted to be wanted. It confuses you, because you think that your feelings were wrong and it makes you feel so small because it's so hard to keep it inside when you let it out and it doesn't coma back. You're left so alone that you can't explain. Damn, there's nothing like that, is there? I've been there and you have too. You're nodding your head."
— Henry Rollins

"Love does not consist of gazing at each other, but in looking outward together in the same direction."
— Antoine de Saint-Exupéry

"I am not sure exactly what heaven will be like, but I know that when we die and it comes time for God to judge us, he will not ask, 'How many good things have you done in your life?' rather he will ask, 'How much love did you put into what you did?"
— Mother Teresa

---

"If he's not calling you, it's because you are not on his mind. If he creates expectations for you, and then doesn't follow through on little things, he will do same for big things. Be aware of this and realize that he's okay with disappointing you. Don't be with someone who doesn't do what they say they're going to do. If he's choosing not to make a simple effort that would put you at ease and bring harmony to a recurring fight, then he doesn't respect your feelings and needs. "Busy" is another word for "asshole." "Asshole" is another word for the guy you're dating. You deserve a fcking phone call."
— Greg Behrendt

"Love is a fire. But whether it is going to warm your hearth or burn down your house, you can never tell."
— Joan Crawford

"I can feel Peeta press his forehead into my temple and he asks, 'So now that you've got me, what are you going to do with me?' I turn into him. 'Put you somewhere you can't get hurt."
— Suzanne Collins

---

"I have something I need to tell you," he says. I run my fingers along the tendons in his hands and look back at him. "I might be in love with you." He smiles a little. "I'm waiting until I'm sure to tell you, though."
"That's sensible of you," I say, smiling too. "We should find some paper so you can make a list or a chart or something."
I feel his laughter against my side, his nose sliding along my jaw, his lips pressing my ear.
"Maybe I'm already sure," he says, "and I just don't want to frighten you."
I laugh a little. "Then you should know better."
"Fine," he says. "Then I love you."
— Veronica Roth

"You are the answer to every prayer I've offered. You are a song, a dream, a whisper, and I don't know how I could have lived without you for as long as I have."
— Nicholas Sparks

"If you remember me,
then I don't care if everyone else forgets."
— Haruki Murakami

"I don't trust people who don't love themselves and
tell me, 'I love you.' ...
There is an African saying which is:
Be careful when a naked person offers you a shirt."
— Maya Angelou

"It was love at first sight, at last sight,
at ever and ever sight."
— Vladimir Nabokov

"Love doesn't just sit there, like a stone, it has to be
made, like bread; remade all the time, made new."
— Ursula K. Le Guin

"We're all seeking that special person who is right for us. But if you've been through enough relationships, you begin to suspect there's no right person, just different flavors of wrong. Why is this? Because you yourself are wrong in some way, and you seek out partners who are wrong in some complementary way. But it takes a lot of living to grow fully into your own wrongness. And it isn't until you finally run up against your deepest demons, your unsolvable problems — the ones that make you truly who you are — that we're ready to find a lifelong mate. Only then do you finally know what you're looking for. You're looking for the wrong person. But not just any wrong person: it's got to be the right wrong person — someone you lovingly gaze upon and think, "This is the problem I want to have."

I will find that special person who is wrong for me in just the right way."

— Andrew Boyd

"And now these three remain: faith, hope and love.
But the greatest of these is love."
— Anonymous

"My dear,
Find what you love and let it kill you.
Let it drain you of your all. Let it cling onto your
back and weigh you down into eventual nothingness.
Let it kill you and let it devour your remains.
For all things will kill you, both slowly and fastly, but
it's much better to be killed by a lover.
~ Falsely yours"
— Charles Bukowski

"If you like her, if she makes you happy, and if you
feel like you know her---then don't let her go."
— Nicholas Sparks

"How many slams in an old screen door? Depends how loud you shut it. How many slices in a bread? Depends how thin you cut it. How much good inside a day? Depends how good you live 'em. How much love inside a friend?
Depends how much you give 'em."
— Shel Silverstein

"If pain must come, may it come quickly. Because I have a life to live, and I need to live it in the best way possible. If he has to make a choice, may he make it now. Then I will either wait for him or forget him."
— Paulo Coelho

"Be careful of love. It'll twist your brain around and leave you thinking up is down and right is wrong."
— Rick Riordan

---

"If you love somebody, let them go, for if they return, they were always yours. If they don't, they never were."
— Kahlil Gibran

"I love you. Remember. They cannot take it"
— Lauren Oliver

"Do you think I'm pretty?
I think you're beautiful
Beautiful?
You are so beautiful, it hurts sometimes."
— Richelle Mead

"I love you more than there are stars in the sky and fish in the sea."
— Nicholas Sparks

---

"When love is not madness it is not love."
— Pedro Calderón de la Barca

"Love does not begin and end the way we seem to think it does. Love is a battle, love is a war; love is a growing up."
— James Baldwin

"A woman's heart should be so hidden in God that a man has to seek Him just to find her."
— Max Lucado

"I cannot fix on the hour, or the spot, or the look or the words, which laid the foundation. It is too long ago. I was in the middle before I knew that I had begun."
— Jane Austen

"Declarations of love amuse me.
Especially when unrequited."
— Cassandra Clare

"True love is rare, and
it's the only thing that gives life real meaning."
— Nicholas Sparks

"What's this?" he demanded, looking from Clary to
his companions, as if they might know what she was
doing there.
"It's a girl," Jace said, recovering his composure.
"Surely you've seen girls before, Alec. Your sister
Isabelle is one."
— Cassandra Clare

"Love is an irresistible desire
to be irresistibly desired."
— Robert Frost

---

"Well, it seems to me that the best relationships - the ones that last - are frequently the ones that are rooted in friendship. You know, one day you look at the person and you see something more than you did the night before. Like a switch has been flicked somewhere. And the person who was just a friend is... suddenly
the only person you can ever imagine yourself
with."
— Gillian Anderson


"I was smiling yesterday, I am smiling today and I will smile tomorrow. Simply because life is too short to cry for anything."
— Santosh Kalwar


"It is good to love many things, for therein lies the true strength, and whosoever loves much performs much, and can accomplish much,
and what is done in love is well done."
— Vincent van Gogh

"Let there be spaces in your togetherness, And let the winds of the heavens dance between you. Love one another but make not a bond of love: Let it rather be a moving sea between the shores of your souls. Fill each other's cup but drink not from one cup. Give one another of your bread but eat not from the same loaf. Sing and dance together and be joyous, but let each one of you be alone, Even as the strings of a lute are alone though they quiver with the same music. Give your hearts, but not into each other's keeping. For only the hand of Life can contain your hearts. And stand together, yet not too near together: For the pillars of the temple stand apart, And the oak tree and the cypress grow not in each other's shadow."
— Kahlil Gibran

"I love you also means I love you more than anyone loves you, or has loved you, or will love you, and also, I love you in a way that no one loves you, or has loved you, or will love you, and also, I love you in a way that I love no one else, and never have loved anyone else, and never will love anyone else."
— Jonathan Safran Foer

"There was a clatter as the basilisk fangs cascaded out of Hermione's arms. Running at Ron, she flung them around his neck and kissed him full on the mouth. Ron threw away the fangs and broomstick he was holding and responded with such enthusiasm that he lifted Hermione off her feet.
"Is this the moment?" Harry asked weakly, and when nothing happened except that Ron and Hermione gripped each other still more firmly and swayed on the spot, he raised his voice. "OI! There's a war going on here!"
Ron and Hermione broke apart, their arms still around each other.
"I know, mate," said Ron, who looked as though he had recently been hit on the back of the head with a Bludger, "so it's now or never, isn't it?"
"Never mind that, what about the Horcrux?" Harry shouted. "D'you think you could just --- just hold it in, until we've got the diadem?"
"Yeah --- right --- sorry ---" said Ron, and he and Hermione set about gathering up fangs, both pink in the face."
— J.K. Rowling

"If I can stop one heart from breaking,
I shall not live in vain."
— Emily Dickinson

"When the power of love overcomes the love of
power, the world will know peace."
— Jimi Hendrix

"I think... if it is true that
there are as many minds as there
are heads, then there are as many
kinds of love as there are hearts."
— Leo Tolstoy

"It is a curious thought, but it is only when you see
people looking ridiculous that you realize just how
much you love them. "
— Agatha Christie

"The greater the love, the greater the tragedy when it's over."
— Nicholas Sparks

"Hate the sin, love the sinner."
— Mahatma Gandhi

"Of all forms of caution, caution in love is perhaps the most fatal to true happiness."
— Bertrand Russell

"One love, one heart, one destiny."
— Bob Marley

"Never close your lips to those whom you have already opened your heart."
— Charles Dickens

"I loved her against reason, against promise, against peace, against hope, against happiness, against all discouragement that could be."
— Charles Dickens

"I fell in love with her courage, her sincerity, and her flaming self respect. And it's these things I'd believe in, even if the whole world indulged in wild suspicions that she wasn't all she should be. I love her and it is the beginning of everything."
— F. Scott Fitzgerald

"If you gave someone your heart and they died, did they take it with them? Did you spend the rest of forever with a hole inside you that couldn't be filled?"
— Jodi Picoult

"It's not the face, but the expressions on it. It's not the voice, but what you say. It's not how you look in that body, but the thing you do with it. You are beautiful."
— Stephenie Meyer

"Well, now
If little by little you stop loving me
I shall stop loving you
Little by little
If suddenly you forget me
Do not look for me
For I shall already have forgotten you

If you think it long and mad the wind of banners that
passes through my life
And you decide to leave me at the shore of the heart
where I have roots
Remember
That on that day, at that hour, I shall lift my arms
And my roots will set off to seek another land"
— Pablo Neruda


"What Is Love? I have met in the streets a very poor
young man who was in love. His hat was old, his
coat worn, the water passed through his shoes and
the stars through his soul"
— Victor Hugo

"You know, when it works, love is pretty amazing. It's not overrated. There's a reason for all those songs."
— Sarah Dessen

"All I ever wanted was to reach out and touch another human being not just with my hands but with my heart."
— Tahereh Mafi

"To me, Fearless is not the absense of fear. It's not being completely unafraid. To me, Fearless is having fears. Fearless is having doubts. Lots of them. To me, Fearless is living in spite of those things that scare you to death."
— Taylor Swift

"I love you like a fat kid loves cake!"
— Scott Adams

"If she's amazing, she won't be easy. If she's easy, she won't be amazing. If she's worth it, you wont give up. If you give up, you're not worthy. ... Truth is, everybody is going to hurt you; you just gotta find the ones worth suffering for."
— Bob Marley

"It isn't possible to love and part. You will wish that it was. You can transmute love, ignore it, muddle it, but you can never pull it out of you. I know by experience that the poets are right: love is eternal."
— E.M. Forster

"We have to allow ourselves to be loved by the people who really love us, the people who really matter. Too much of the time, we are blinded by our own pursuits of people to love us, people that don't even matter, while all that time we waste and the people who do love us have to stand on the sidewalk and watch us beg in the streets! It's time to put an end to this. It's time for us to let ourselves be loved."
— C. JoyBell C.

"Gravitation is not responsible for
people falling in love."
— Albert Einstein


"We waste time looking for the perfect lover, instead
of creating the perfect love."
— Tom Robbins


"They say when you are missing someone that they
are probably feeling the same, but I don't think it's
possible for you to miss me as much as I'm missing
you right now"
— Edna St. Vincent Millay


"And when her lips met mine, I knew that I could
live to be a hundred and visit every country in the
world, but nothing would ever compare to that single
moment when I first kissed the girl of my dreams
and knew that my love would last forever."
— Nicholas Sparks

"Any fool can be happy. It takes a man with real
heart to make beauty out of the stuff
that makes us weep."
— Clive Barker

"Welcome to the wonderful world of jealousy, he
thought. For the price of admission, you get a
splitting headache, a nearly irresistable urge to
commit murder,
and an inferiority complex. Yippee."
— J.R. Ward

"What is hell? I maintain that it is the suffering of
being unable to love."
— Fyodor Dostoyevsky

"You couldn't relive your life, skipping the awful
parts, without losing what made it worthwhile. You
had to accept it as a whole--like the world, or the
person you loved."
— Stewart O'Nan

"The most painful thing is losing yourself in the
process of loving someone too much, and forgetting
that you are special too."
— Ernest Hemingway

"Love is not affectionate feeling, but a steady wish
for the loved person's ultimate good
as far as it can be obtained."
— C.S. Lewis

"Life, he realize, was much like a song. In the
beginning there is mystery, in the end there is
confirmation, but it's in the middle where all the
emotion resides to make the whole thing
worthwhile."
— Nicholas Sparks

"Find what you love and let it kill you."
— Charles Bukowski

"It's probably not just by chance that I'm alone. It would be very hard for a man to live with me, unless he's terribly strong. And if he's stronger than I, I'm the one who can't live with him. … I'm neither smart nor stupid, but I don't think I'm a run-of-the-mill person. I've been in business without being a businesswoman, I've loved without being a woman made only for love. The two men I've loved, I think, will remember me, on earth or in heaven, because men always remember a woman who caused them concern and uneasiness. I've done my best, in regard to people and to life, without precepts, but with a taste for justice."
— Coco Chanel

"Love is an untamed force. When we try to control it, it destroys us. When we try to imprison it, it enslaves us. When we try to understand it, it leaves us feeling lost and confused."
— Paulo Coelho

"Love is a temporary madness, it erupts like volcanoes and then subsides. And when it subsides, you have to make a decision. You have to work out whether your roots have so entwined together that it is inconceivable that you should ever part. Because this is what love is. Love is not breathlessness, it is not excitement, it is not the promulgation of promises of eternal passion, it is not the desire to mate every second minute of the day, it is not lying awake at night imagining that he is kissing every cranny of your body. No, don't blush, I am telling you some truths. That is just being "in love", which any fool can do. Love itself is what is left over when being in love has burned away, and this is both an art and a fortunate accident."
— Louis de Bernières

"The man of knowledge must be able not only to love his enemies but also to hate his friends."
— Friedrich Nietzsche

---

"Things we lose have a way of coming back to us in
the end, if not always in the way we expect."
— J.K. Rowling

"Look after my heart - I've left it with you."
— Stephenie Meyer

"One cannot think well, love well, sleep well,
if one has not dined well."
— Virginia Woolf

"I would like to be the air that inhabits you for a
moment only. I would like to be
that unnoticed and that necessary."
— Margaret Atwood

"And then he gives me a smile that just seems so
genuinely sweet with just the right touch of shyness
that unexpected warmth rushes through me."
— Suzanne Collins

"I want to do with you
what spring does with the cherry trees."
— Pablo Neruda

"He does something to me, that boy. Every time. It's
his only detriment. He steps on my heart. He makes
me cry."
— Markus Zusak

"Have enough courage to trust love one more time
and always one more time."
— Maya Angelou

"You can't measure the mutual affection of two
human beings by the number of words they
exchange."
— Milan Kundera

---

"Before you, Bella, my life was like a moonless night.
Very dark, but there were stars, points of light and
reason. ...And then you shot across my sky like a
meteor. Suddenly everything was on fire; there was
brilliancy, there was beauty. When you were gone,
when the meteor had fallen over the horizon,
everything went black. Nothing had changed, but my
eyes were blinded by the light.
I couldn't see the stars anymore.
And there was no more reason, for anything."
— Stephenie Meyer

"Sometimes it's a form of love just to talk to
somebody that you have nothing in common with
and still be fascinated by their presence."
— David Byrne

"Tonight I can write the saddest lines
I loved her, and sometimes she loved me too."
— Pablo Neruda

"How do you spell 'love'?" - Piglet
"You don't spell it...you feel it." - Pooh"
— A.A. Milne


"I crave your mouth, your voice, your hair.
Silent and starving, I prowl through the streets.
Bread does not nourish me, dawn disrupts me, all
day
I hunt for the liquid measure of your steps.

I hunger for your sleek laugh,
your hands the color of a savage harvest,
hunger for the pale stones of your fingernails,
I want to eat your skin like a whole almond.

I want to eat the sunbeam flaring in your lovely
body,
the sovereign nose of your arrogant face,
I want to eat the fleeting shade of your lashes,

and I pace around hungry, sniffing the twilight,
hunting for you, for your hot heart,
Like a puma in the barrens of Quitratue."
— Pablo Neruda

"Letting go doesn't mean that you don't care about someone anymore. It's just realizing that the only person you really have control over is yourself."
— Deborah Reber

"Happiness [is] only real when shared"
— Jon Krakauer

"A DEFINITION NOT FOUND
IN THE DICTIONARY
Not leaving: an act of trust and love,
often deciphered by children"
— Markus Zusak

"One day you will kiss a man you can't breathe without, and find that breath is of little consequence."
— Karen Marie Moning

---

"Maybe...you'll fall in love with me all over again."
"Hell," I said, "I love you enough now. What do you
want to do? Ruin me?'
"Yes. I want to ruin you."
"Good," I said. "That's what I want too."
— Ernest Hemingway


"Was it hard?" I ask.
Letting go?"
Not as hard as holding on to something
that wasn't real."
— Lisa Schroeder


"I'm saying that I'm a moody, insecure, narrow-
minded, jealous, borderline homicidal bitch, and I
want you to promise me that you're okay with that,
because it's who I am, and you're what I need."
— Jeaniene Frost

"Then I realize what it is. It's him. Something about him makes me feel like I am about to fall. Or turn to liquid. Or burst into flames."
— Veronica Roth

"As if you were on fire from within.
The moon lives in the lining of your skin."
— Pablo Neruda

"The beginning of love is the will to let those we love be perfectly themselves, the resolution not to twist them to fit our own image. If in loving them we do not love what they are, but only their potential likeness to ourselves, then we do not love them: we only love the reflection of ourselves
we find in them"
— Thomas Merton

---

""Promise me you'll never forget me because if I
thought you would, I'd never leave."
— A.A. Milne

"Anyone who falls in love is searching for the
missing pieces of themselves. So anyone who's in
love gets sad when they think of their lover. It's like
stepping back inside a room you have fond memories
of, one you haven't seen in a long time."
— Haruki Murakami

"Art and love are the same thing: It's the process of
seeing yourself in things that are not you."
— Chuck Klosterman

"I wasn't actually in love,
but I felt a sort of tender curiosity."
— F. Scott Fitzgerald

---

"I could not tell you if I loved you the first moment I saw you, or if it was the second or third or fourth. But I remember the first moment I looked at you walking toward me and realized that somehow the rest of the world seemed to vanish when I was with you."
— Cassandra Clare

"When I am with you, we stay up all night. When you're not here, I can't go to sleep. Praise God for those two insomnias! And the difference between them."
— Jalaluddin Rumi

"I loved you like a man loves a woman he never touches, only writes to, keeps little photographs of."
— Charles Bukowski

"You yourself, as much as anybody in the entire universe, deserve your love and affection"
— Sharon Salzberg

"Tears shed for another person are not a sign of weakness. They are a sign of a pure heart."
— José N. Harris

"The saddest people I've ever met in life are the ones who don't care deeply about anything at all. Passion and satisfaction go hand in hand, and without them, any happiness is only temporary, because there's nothing to make it last."
— Nicholas Sparks

"If conversation was the lyrics, laughter was the music, making time spent together a melody that could be replayed over and over without getting stale."
— Nicholas Sparks

"She leaned down and looked at his lifeless face and Leisel kissed her best friend, Rudy Steiner, soft and true on his lips. He tasted dusty and sweet. He tasted like regret in the shadows of trees and in the glow of the anarchist's suit collection. She kissed him long and soft, and when she pulled herself away, she touched his mouth with her fingers...She did not say goodbye. She was incapable, and after a few more minutes at his side, she was able to tear herself from the ground. It amazes me what humans can do, even when streams are flowing down their faces and they stagger on..."
— Markus Zusak

"You could have fooled me. Everytime I called you, Luke said you were sick.
I figured you were avoiding me. Again."
"I wasn't. I did want to talk to you. I've been thinking about you all the time."
"I've been thinking about you, too."
"I really was sick. I swear.
I almost died back there on the ship, you know."
"I know. Everytime you almost die, I almost die myself."
— Cassandra Clare

"We are all alone, born alone, die alone, and—in spite of True Romance magazines—we shall all someday look back on our lives and see that, in spite of our company, we were alone the whole way. I do not say lonely—at least, not all the time—but essentially, and finally, alone. This is what makes your self-respect so important, and I don't see how you can respect yourself if you must look in the hearts and minds of others for your happiness."
— Hunter S. Thompson


"It is the time you have wasted for your rose that makes your rose so important."
— Antoine de Saint-Exupéry


"I fell in love with him. But I don't just stay with him by default as if there's no one else available to me. I stay with him because I choose to, every day that I wake up, every day that we fight or lie to each other or disappoint each other. I choose him over and over again, and he chooses me."
— Veronica Roth

"In time, the hurt began to fade and it was easier to just let it go. At least I thought it was. But in every boy I met in the next few years, I found myself looking for you, and when the feelings got too strong, I'd write you another letter. But I never sent them for fear of what I might find. By then, you'd gone on with your life and I didn't want to think about you loving someone else. I wanted to remember us like we were that summer. I didn't ever want to lose that."
— Nicholas Sparks

"There is only one page left to write on. I will fill it with words of only one syllable. I love.
I have loved. I will love."
— Audrey Niffenegger

"Happiness is holding someone in your arms and knowing you hold the whole world."
— Orhan Pamuk

"Sometimes when I look at you,
I feel I'm gazing at a distant star.
It's dazzling, but the light is from tens of thousands
of years ago.
Maybe the star doesn't even exist any more. Yet
sometimes that light seems more real to me than
anything."
— Haruki Murakami


"A half-read book is a half-finished love affair."
— David Mitchell


"To love oneself is the beginning
of a lifelong romance."
— Oscar Wilde


"Someone I loved once gave me a box full of
darkness. It took me years to understand
that this too, was a gift."
— Mary Oliver

---

"I like flaws. I think they make things interesting."
— Sarah Dessen

"I'm oxygen and he's dying to breathe."
— Tahereh Mafi

"Who, being loved, is poor?"
— Oscar Wilde

"Lost love is still love. It takes a different form, that's all. You can't see their smile or bring them food or tousle their hair or move them around a dance floor. But when those senses weaken another heightens. Memory. Memory becomes your partner. You nurture it. You hold it. You dance with it."
— Mitch Albom

"I read once that the ancient Egyptians had fifty words for sand & the Eskimos had a hundred words for snow. I wish I had a thousand words for love, but all that comes to mind is the way you move against me while you sleep & there are no words for that."
— Brian Andreas

"Every one of us is, in the cosmic perspective, precious. If a human disagrees with you, let him live. In a hundred billion galaxies, you will not find another."
— Carl Sagan

"I'm not sentimental--I'm as romantic as you are. The idea, you know, is that the sentimental person thinks things will last-- the romantic person has a desperate confidence that they won't."
— F. Scott Fitzgerald

---

"I'm on Aslan's side even if there isn't any Aslan to lead it. I'm going to live as like a Narnian as I can even if there isn't any Narnia."
— C.S. Lewis

"Peeta, how come I never know when you're having a nightmare?" I say.

"I don't know. I don't think I cry out or thrash around or anything. I just come to, paralyzed with terror," he says.

"You should wake me," I say, thinking about how I can interrupt his sleep two or three times on a bad night. About how long it can take to calm me down.

"It's not necessary. My nightmares are usually about losing you," he says. "I'm okay once I realize you're here."
— Suzanne Collins

"A purpose of human life, no matter who is
controlling it, is to love
whoever is around to be loved."
— Kurt Vonnegut Jr.

"It is easy to love people in memory; the hard thing is
to love them when they are there in front of you."
— John Updike

"The reason it hurts so much to separate is because
our souls are connected. Maybe they always have
been and will be. Maybe we've lived a thousand lives
before this one and in each of them we've found each
other. And maybe each time, we've been forced apart
for the same reasons. That means that this goodbye is
both a goodbye for the past ten thousand years and a
prelude to what will come."
— Nicholas Sparks

---

"Love can change a person the way a parent can
change a baby- awkwardly,
and often with a great deal of mess."
— Lemony Snicket

"When I saw you I fell in love, and you smiled
because you knew."
— Arrigo Boito

"You know how they say you only hurt the ones you
love? Well, it works both ways."
— Chuck Palahniuk

"Be with me always - take any form - drive me mad!
only do not leave me in this abyss, where I cannot
find you! Oh, God! it is unutterable! I can not live
without my life! I can not live without my soul!"
— Emily Brontë

---

"I fell in love with her when we were together, then
fell deeper in love with her
in the years we were apart."
— Nicholas Sparks

"I know we're fucked up, alright? I'm impulsive, and
hot tempered, and you get under my skin like no one
else. You act like you hate me one minute, and then
need me the next. I never get anything right, and I
don't deserve you...but I fucking love you, Abby. I
love you more than I loved anyone or anything ever.
When you're around, I don't need booze, or money,
or the fighting, or the one-night stands..."
— Jamie McGuire

"What she had realized was that love was that
moment when your heart was about to burst."
— Stieg Larsson

---

"Sorrow is how we learn to love. Your heart isn't breaking. It hurts because it's getting larger. The larger it gets, the more love it holds."
— Rita Mae Brown

"Sorrow is how we learn to love. Your heart isn't breaking. It hurts because it's getting larger. The larger it gets, the more love it holds."
— Rita Mae Brown

"One word
Frees us of all the weight and pain of life:
That word is love."
— Sophocles

"Respect was invented to cover the empty place where love should be."
— Leo Tolstoy

"Yes, I was infatuated with you: I am still. No one has ever heightened such a keen capacity of physical sensation in me. I cut you out because I couldn't stand being a passing fancy. Before I give my body, I must give my thoughts, my mind, my dreams. And you weren't having any of those."
— Sylvia Plath

"It takes courage to love, but pain through love is the purifying fire which those who love generously know. We all know people who are so much afraid of pain that they shut themselves up like clams in a shell and, giving out nothing, receive nothing and therefore shrink until life is a mere living death."
— Eleanor Roosevelt

"I guess that's just part of loving people: You have to give things up. Sometimes you even have to give them up."
— Lauren Oliver

---

"I will love you always. When this red hair is white, I will still love you. When the smooth softness of youth is replaced by the delicate softness of age, I will still want to touch your skin. When your face is full of the lines of every smile you have ever smiled, of every surprise I have seen flash through your eyes, when every tear you have ever cried has left its mark upon your face,I will treasure you all the more, because I was there to see it all. I will share your life with you, Meredith, and I will love you until the last breath leaves your body or mine."
— Laurell K. Hamilton


"The more one judges, the less one loves."
— Honoré de Balzac


"The heart has its reasons which reason knows not."
— Blaise Pascal

"The emotion that can break your heart is sometimes
the very one that heals it..."
— Nicholas Sparks

"Trust your heart if the seas catch fire, live by love
though the stars walk backward."
— E.E. Cummings

"Do not fall in love with people like me.
I will take you to museums, and parks, and
monuments, and kiss you in every beautiful place, so
that you can never go back to them without tasting
me like blood in your mouth.
I will destroy you in the most beautiful way possible.
And when I leave you will finally understand, why
storms are named after people."
— Caitlyn Siehl

---

"Sometimes love means letting go
when you want to hold on tighter."
— Melissa Marr

"Holding Eleanor's hand was like holding a butterfly.
Or a heartbeat. Like holding something complete,
and completely alive."
— Rainbow Rowell

"Time was passing like a hand waving from a train I
wanted to be on.
I hope you never have to think about anything as
much as I think about you."
— Jonathan Safran Foer

"The love of learning, the sequestered nooks,
And all the sweet serenity of books"
— Henry Wadsworth Longfellow

"If someone were to harm my family or a friend or somebody I love, I would eat them. I might end up in jail for 500 years, but I would eat them."
— Johnny Depp

"From childhood's hour I have not been. As others were, I have not seen. As others saw, I could not awaken. My heart to joy at the same tone. And all I loved, I loved alone."
— Edgar Allan Poe

"Come sleep with me:
We won't make Love, Love will make us."
— Julio Cortázar

"People have forgotten this truth," the fox said. "But you mustn't forget it. You become responsible forever for what you've tamed.
You're responsible for your rose."
— Antoine de Saint-Exupéry

"If you stay, I'll do whatever you want. I'll quit the band, go with you to New York. But if you need me to go away, I'll do that, too. I was talking to Liz and she said maybe coming back to your old life would be too painful, that maybe it'd be easier for you to erase us. And that would suck, but I'd do it. I can lose you like that if I don't lose you today. I'll let you go. If you stay."
— Gayle Forman, If I Stay

"Nothing takes the taste out of peanut butter quite like unrequited love."
— Charles M. Schulz

---

"When someone is in your heart, they're never truly gone. They can come back to you, even at unlikely times."
— Mitch Albom

"Ever has it been that love knows not its own depth until the hour of separation."
— Kahlil Gibran

"Don't cry over someone who wouldn't cry over you."
— Lauren Conrad

"Absence diminishes small loves and increases great ones, as the wind blows out the candle and fans the bonfire."
— François de La Rochefoucauld

"Being with you never felt wrong. It's the one thing I did right. You're the one thing I did right."
— Becca Fitzpatrick

"I wonder how many people don't get the one they want, but end up with the one they're supposed to be with."
— Fannie Flagg

"How do I love thee? Let me count the ways.
I love thee to the depth and breadth and height
My soul can reach"
— Elizabeth Barrett Browning

"When you trip over love, it is easy to get up. But when you fall in love,
it is impossible to stand again."
— Albert Einstein

"This is where it all begins.
Everything starts here, today."
— David Nicholls


"to love life, to love it even
when you have no stomach for it
and everything you've held dear
crumbles like burnt paper in your hands,
your throat filled with the silt of it.
When grief sits with you, its tropical heat
thickening the air, heavy as water
more fit for gills than lungs;
when grief weights you like your own flesh
only more of it, an obesity of grief,
you think, How can a body withstand this?
Then you hold life like a face
between your palms, a plain face,
no charming smile, no violet eyes,
and you say, yes, I will take you
I will love you, again."
— Ellen Bass

---

"Without you in my arms, I feel emptiness in my soul. I find myself searching the crowds for your face
- I know it's impossibility,
but I cannot help myself."
— Nicholas Sparks

"To be fully seen by somebody, then, and be loved anyhow - this is a human offering
that can border on miraculous."
— Elizabeth Gilbert

"I've been fighting to be who I am all my life. What's the point of being who I am, if I can't have the person who was worth all the fighting for?"
— Stephanie Lennox

"I want to be in a relationship where you telling me you love me is just a ceremonious validation of what you already show me."
— Steve Maraboli

"In your light I learn how to love. In your beauty, how to make poems. You dance inside my chest where no-one sees you, but sometimes I do, and that sight becomes this art."
— Jalaluddin Rumi

"The power of a glance has been so much abused in love stories, that it has come to be disbelieved in. Few people dare now to say that two beings have fallen in love because they have looked at each other. Yet it is in this way that love begins, and in this way only."
— Victor Hugo

"We're staying together," he promised. "You're not getting away from me. Never again."
— Rick Riordan

---

"You'll get over it…" It's the clichés that cause the trouble. To lose someone you love is to alter your life for ever. You don't get over it because 'it" is the person you loved. The pain stops, there are new people, but the gap never closes. How could it? The particularness of someone who mattered enough to grieve over is not made anodyne by death. This hole in my heart is in the shape of you and no-one else can fit it. Why would I want them to?"
— Jeanette Winterson

"Watch out for intellect,
because it knows so much it knows nothing
and leaves you hanging upside down,
mouthing knowledge as your heart
falls out of your mouth."
— Anne Sexton

"True love is usually the most inconvenient kind."
— Kiera Cass

"We're staying together," he promised. "You're not getting away from me. Never again."
— Rick Riordan

"The sunlight claps the earth, and the moonbeams kiss the sea: what are all these kissings worth, if thou kiss not me?"
— Percy Bysshe Shelley

"Even
After
All this time
The Sun never says to the Earth,

"You owe me."

Look
What happens
With a love like that,
It lights the whole sky."
— Hafiz

"When I say it's you I like, I'm talking about that part of you that knows that life is far more than anything you can ever see or hear or touch. That deep part of you that allows you to stand for those things without which humankind cannot survive. Love that conquers hate, peace that rises triumphant over war, and justice that proves more powerful than greed."
— Fred Rogers

"To lose balance sometimes for love is part of living a balanced life."
— Elizabeth Gilbert

"You know it's never fifty-fifty in a marriage. It's always seventy-thirty, or sixty-forty. Someone falls in love first. Someone puts someone else up on a pedestal. Someone works very hard to keep things rolling smoothly;
someone else sails along for the ride."
— Jodi Picoult

"If you love something set it free, but don't be surprised if it comes back with herpes."
— Chuck Palahniuk

"My wish is that you may be loved to the point of madness."
— André Breton

"The things we love destroy us every time, lad. Remember that."
— George R.R. Martin

"Throw your dreams into space like a kite, and you do not know what it will bring back, a new life, a new friend, a new love, a new country."
— Anaïs Nin

"I sought to hear the voice of God and climbed the topmost steeple, but God declared: "Go down again - I dwell among the people."
— John Henry Newman

"The bond forged between us was not one that could be broken by absence, distance, or time. And no matter how much more special or beautiful or brilliant or perfect than me he might be, he was as irreversibly altered as I was. As I would always belong to him, so would he always be mine."
— Stephenie Meyer

"If we have no peace, it is because we have forgotten that we belong to each other."
— Mother Teresa

"sometimes you don't need a goal in life, you don't need to know the big picture. you just need to know what you're going to do next!"
— Sophie Kinsella

"We are who we are, because of those we choose to love and because of those who love us."
— Kate Mosse

"I won't ever leave you, even though you're always leaving me."
— Audrey Niffenegger

"This is what we call love. When you are loved, you can do anything in creation. When you are loved, there's no need at all to understand what's happening, because everything happens within you."
— Paulo Coelho

---

"The course of true love never did run smooth."
— William Shakespeare

"I love you as certain dark things are loved, secretly,
between the shadow and the soul."
— Stephanie Perkins

"The only calibration that counts is how much heart
people invest, how much they ignore their fears of
being hurt or caught out or humiliated. And the only
thing people regret is that they didn't live boldly
enough, that they didn't invest enough heart, didn't
love enough. Nothing else really counts at all."
— Ted Hughes

---

"Sometimes when I'm alone, I take the pearl from
where it lives in my pocket and try to remember the
boy with the bread, the strong arms that warded off
nightmares on the train, the kisses in the arena."
— Suzanne Collins

"We are not trapped or locked up in these bones. No,
no. We are free to change. And love changes us. And
if we can love one another,
we can break open the sky."
— Walter Mosley

"You have to kiss a lot of frogs
before you find your prince"
— E.L. James

"I'm about to make a wild, extreme and severe relationship rule: the word busy is a load of crap and is most often used by assholes. The word "busy" is the relationship Weapon of Mass Destruction. It seems like a good excuse, but in fact in every silo you uncover, all you're going to find is a man who didn't care enough to call. Remember men are never to busy to get what they want."
— Greg Behrendt

"About all you can do in life is be who you are. Some people will love you for you. Most will love you for what you can do for them, and some won't like you at all."
— Rita Mae Brown

"For my part, I prefer my heart to be broken. It is so lovely, dawn-kaleidoscopic within the crack."
— D.H. Lawrence

"The world was collapsing, and the only thing that really mattered to me was that she was alive."
— Rick Riordan

"When I look in the mirror, I know I'm looking at someone who isn't sure
she deserves to be loved at all."
— Nicholas Sparks

"I was always hungry for love. Just once, I wanted to know what it was like to get my fill of it -- to be fed so much love I couldn't take any more. Just once. "
— Haruki Murakami

"Romance is the glamour which turns the dust of everyday life into a golden haze. "
— Elinor Glyn

"Ok. You fuck me, then snub me. You love me, you hate me. You show me a sensitive side, then you turn into a total asshole. Is this a pretty accurate description of our relationship."
— Chuck Palahniuk

"In a perfect world, you could fuck people without giving them a piece of your heart. And every glittering kiss and every touch of flesh is another shard of heart you'll never see again."
— Neil Gaiman

---

"If there is no love in the world, we will make a new world, and we will give it walls, and we will furnish it with soft, red interiors, from the inside out, and give it a knocker that resonates like a diamond falling to a jeweller's felt so that we should never hear it. Love me, because love doesn't exist, and I have tried everything that does."
— Jonathan Safran Foer

"For where all love is, the speaking is unnecessary"
— Diana Gabaldon

"The human heart is a strange vessel. Love and hatred can exist side by side."
— Scott Westerfeld

---

"Someday you're gonna look back on this moment of your life as such a sweet time of grieving. You'll see that you were in mourning and your heart was broken, but your life was changing..."
— Elizabeth Gilbert

"When we meet someone and fall in love, we have a sense that the whole universe is on our side. And yet if something goes wrong, there is nothing left! How is it possible for the beauty that was there only minutes before to vanish so quickly? Life moves very fast. It rushes from heaven to hell in a matter of seconds."
— Paulo Coelho

"sex is the consolation you have when you can't have love"
— Gabriel García Márquez

"Spending time with you showed me what I've been
missing in my life."
— Nicholas Sparks

"In the moment when I truly understand my enemy,
understand him well enough to defeat him, then in
that very moment I also love him. I think it's
impossible to really understand somebody, what
they want, what they believe, and not love them the
way they love themselves. And then, in that very
moment when I love them.... I destroy them."
— Orson Scott Card

"It is possible to be in love with you
just because of who you are."
— Maggie Stiefvater

"If he loved with all the powers of his puny being, he
couldn't love as much in eighty years
as I could in a day."
— Emily Brontë

"The music in his laughter had a way of rounding off
the missing notes in her soul."
— Gloria Naylor


"O Romeo, Romeo, wherefore art thou Romeo?
Deny thy father refuse thy name, thou art thyself
thou not a montegue, what is montegue? tis nor hand
nor foot nor any other part belonging to a man
What is in a name?
That which we call a rose by any other name would
smell as sweet,
So Romeo would were he not Romeo called retain
such dear perfection to which he owes without that
title,
Romeo, Doth thy name!
And for that name which is no part of thee, take all
thyself."
— William Shakespeare

"Even more, I had never meant to love him. One thing I truly knew - knew it in the pit of my stomach, in the center of my bones, knew it from the crown of my head to the soles of my feet, knew it deep in my empty chest - was how love gave someone the power to break you"
— Stephenie Meyer

"I bet you could sometimes find all the mysteries of the universe in someone's hand."
— Benjamin Alire Sáenz

"More smiling, less worrying. More compassion, less judgment. More blessed, less stressed.
More love, less hate."
— Roy T. Bennett

"Yet each man kills the thing he loves
By each let this be heard
Some do it with a bitter look
Some with a flattering word
The coward does it with a kiss
The brave man with a sword"
— Oscar Wilde

"Each of us is born with a box of matches inside us
but we can't strike them all by ourselves"
— Laura Esquivel

"If only she could be so oblivious again, to feel such
love without knowing it, mistaking it for laughter."
— Markus Zusak

"I know that's what people say-- you'll get over it. I'd say it, too. But I know it's not true. Oh, youll be happy again, never fear. But you won't forget. Every time you fall in love it will be because something in the man reminds you of him."
— Betty Smith

"Love is a decision, it is a judgment, it is a promise. If love were only a feeling, there would be no basis for the promise to love each other forever. A feeling comes and it may go. How can I judge that it will stay forever, when my act does not involve judgment and decision."
— Erich Fromm

"I'd learned that some things are best kept secret."
— Nicholas Sparks

"But love is always new. Regardless of whether we love once, twice, or a dozen times in our life, we always face a brand-new situation. Love can consign us to hell or to paradise, but it always takes us somewhere. We simply have to accept it, because it is what nourishes our existence. If we reject it, we die of hunger, because we lack the courage to stretch out a hand and pluck the fruit from the branches of the tree of life. We have to take love where we find it, even if that means hours, days, weeks
of disappointment and sadness.
The moment we begin to seek love, love begins to seek us. And to save us."
— Paulo Coelho

"I almost wish we were butterflies and liv'd but three summer days - three such days with you I could fill with more delight than fifty common years could ever contain."
— John Keats

"I know enough to know that no woman should ever marry a man who hated his mother."
— Martha Gellhorn

"You're in a car with a beautiful boy, and he won't tell you that he loves you, but he loves you. And you feel like you've done something terrible, like robbed a liquor store, or swallowed pills, or shoveled yourself a grave in the dirt, and you're tired. You're in a car with a beautiful boy, and you're trying not to tell him that you love him, and you're trying to choke down the feeling, and you're trembling, but he reaches over and he touches you, like a prayer for which no words exist, and you feel your heart taking root in your body, like you've discovered something you didn't even have a name for."
— Richard Siken

"Love is how you stay alive,
even after you are gone."
— Mitch Albom

"I am not an angel,' I asserted; 'and I will not be one
till I die: I will be myself. Mr. Rochester, you must
neither expect nor exact anything celestial of me - for
you will not get it, any more than I shall get it of you:
which I do not at all anticipate."
— Charlotte Brontë

"love, I've come to understand is more than three
words mumbled before bedtime."
— Nicholas Sparks

---

"It's not how much we give
but how much love we put into giving."
— Mother Teresa

"The highest function of love is that it makes the
loved one a unique and irreplaceable being."
— Tom Robbins

"We are told that people stay in love because of
chemistry, or because they remain intrigued with
each other, because of many kindnesses, because of
luck. But part of it has got to be forgiveness
and gratefulness. "
— Ellen Goodman

"Don't waste your love on somebody,
who doesn't value it."
— William Shakespeare

"NO. No no no. I don't want to screw you. I just love
you. When did who you want to screw become the
whole game? Since when is the person you want to
screw the only person you get to love? It's so stupid,
Tiny! I mean, Jesus, who even gives a fuck about
sex?! People act like it's the most important thing
humans do, but come on. How can our sentient
fucking lives revolve around something slugs can do.
I mean, who you want to screw and whether you
screw them? Those are important questions, I guess.
But they're not that important. You know what's
important? Who would you die for? Who do you
wake up at five forty-five in the morning for even
though you don't even know why he needs you?
Whose drunken nose would you pick?!"
— John Green

"And next time you're planning to injure yourself to get me attention, just remember that a little sweet talk works wonders."
— Cassandra Clare

"And what would humans be without love?"
RARE, said Death."
— Terry Pratchett

"Afterward, I had the last laugh. I made an air bubble at the bottom of the lake. Our friends kept waiting for us to come up, but hey-when you are the son of Poseidon, you don't have to hurry. And it was pretty much the best underwater kiss of all time."
— Rick Riordan

---



"Love is not the absence of logic
but logic examined and recalculated
heated and curved to fit
inside the contours of the heart"
— Tammara Webber

"The soul is healed by being with children."
— Fyodor Dostoyevsky

"True love is not so much a matter of romance as it is
a matter of anxious concern for the well-being of
one's companion."
— Gordon B. Hinckley

"I have feelings too. I am still human. All I want is to be loved, for myself and for my talent. "
— Marilyn Monroe

"Sometimes God allows what he hates to accomplish what he loves."
— Joni Eareckson Tada

"Hearts are breakable," Isabelle said. "And I think even when you heal, you're never what you were before"."
— Cassandra Clare

www.ingramcontent.com/pod-product-compliance
Lightning Source LLC
Chambersburg PA
CBHW070813260726
48660CB00005B/1836